Island

Also by Douglas Walbourne-Gough

Crow Gulch

ISLAND

Douglas Walbourne-Gough

icehouse poetry
an imprint of Goose Lane Editions

Edited by Sue Sinclair.
Cover and page design by Julie Scriver.
Cover image derived from "Moose antler at Tablelands in Gros Morne National Park, Newfoundland" on Wikimedia Commons, CC BY-SA 2.0.
Interior cover images courtesy of Douglas Walbourne-Gough.
Printed in Canada by HUME Media.
10 9 8 7 6 5 4 3

Library and Archives Canada Cataloguing in Publication

Title: Island / Douglas Walbourne-Gough.
Names: Walbourne-Gough, Douglas, 1982- author.
Identifiers: Canadiana (print) 20240355199 | Canadiana (ebook) 20240358449 | ISBN 9781773103396 (softcover) | ISBN 9781773104430 (EPUB)
Subjects: LCGFT: Poetry.
Classification: LCC PS8645.A4555 I85 2024 | DDC C811/.6—dc23

Goose Lane Editions acknowledges the generous support of the Government of Canada, the Canada Council for the Arts, and the Government of New Brunswick.

Goose Lane Editions is located on the unceded territory of the Wəlastəkwiyik whose ancestors along with the Mi'kmaq and Peskotomuhkati Nations signed Peace and Friendship Treaties with the British Crown in the 1700s.

Goose Lane Editions
500 Beaverbrook Court, Suite 330
Fredericton, New Brunswick
CANADA E3B 5X4
gooselane.com

This book is dedicated to Elder Calvin White.
Wela'lin for your generosity of time, wisdom, honesty, and friendship.

And his hands?
His hands keep turning into birds and
flying away from him. *Him being you.*
Yes. *Do you love yourself?* I don't have to
answer that.

— Richard Siken

Could you have sympathetic feelings in more than one direction? And can you think at the same time?

— Mary Ruefle

Division

My family got a letter from the Federation of Newfoundland Indians, stating that we were part of a class-action lawsuit. FNI was going to fight for us. A few months before that, Canada rejected our applications for enrolment in the Qalipu First Nation. Initially, I was relieved by the rejection. I'd watched my hometown divide itself — are you Mi'kmaq or settler? Mi'kmaq or not Mi'kmaq enough? Do you want tax off your truck, or do you want to decolonize, reconnect with who and where you come from? Or have you known yourself all along and no one, federal or local, gets to tell you otherwise?

As a community, we became suspicious of eye and hair colour, felt economic jealousies when a neighbour was finally able to access dental care, get glasses for their kids, afford medication. I heard the jeers about the whole southwest coast suddenly having free university, every mouth full of gold teeth, dripping with self-entitlement.

During the Qalipu enrolment process, I worked at the public library in Corner Brook. I witnessed people who, only months before, asked each other, *How's the family?* People who chatted weather, recommended each other good books. Now, they interrogated each other's surnames, places of birth. So engaged in more-status-than-thou that we missed the point entirely — we were already doing the government's dirty work, tearing each other down when we most needed to build each other up.

I very nearly kept my name out of the FNI lawsuit. I was tempted to avoid facing the struggle with my identity, Indigeneity, self-doubts. The doubts and disbelief of others, both perceived and real. I'd buried the *Crow Gulch* manuscript for over a year out of that same anxiety.

Perhaps we forgot, or never even knew, about the Mi'kmaq in Flat Bay, who, decades before I was born, fought to be federally recognized, to be taken seriously as Indigenous Newfoundlanders at a time when we were dismissed as myth, seen with indifference at best. We likely never asked ourselves, *How does the Mi'kmaq Grand Council feel about this?* Neither did the federal government. No wonder none of us felt we could trust each other. Ottawa got to put its feet up, watch us propagate our own division.

I know I don't have all the details, but neither do you, or any of us just yet. That picture only becomes clearer when we sit and truly listen to each other. All I can write is what I've seen, felt, and experienced, and hope that helps. Recognize the gaps in my knowledge, slowly fill them in as I reckon with centuries of colonization while figuring out what a Newfoundland Indigeneity is, what it can be. There is beauty, love, and power in our potential.

If I can't employ humility, can't be honest about how there's no flicked switch from Newfoundlander to Mi'kmaq, then I do disservice to my grandmothers. I do disservice to the Elders and scholars I've met and read so far and the ones ahead. I do disservice to other Newfoundlanders, Indigenous or not, who might not know where they stand. Who might not know how to feel about these Indigenous Newfoundland voices and faces now making room for themselves on this island, in this country, finally feeling some sort of permission to say, *I exist*.

Contents

Another Visit from My Grandfather 13
Guilt 14
Corner Brook 16
This All Happened? 18
I Didn't Just Let This Happen 22
I Visit Margie with Moose Meat 23
Childhood Photo 24
I Didn't Just Let This Happen 25
The Waves 26
Ten Percent 28
Steep Steps toward Home 29
I Didn't Just Let This Happen 31
Or Perhaps You Have 32
My Uncouth Mouth 34
I Visit My Grandfather with Sea Trout 37
I Didn't Just Let This Happen 38
Canada's Happy Province 39
Safety 40
Housewarming 41
The Believer's Daily Planner: *July 23, 1989–July 22, 1990* 42
Herd 44
I Didn't Just Let This Happen 45
Attention 46
At Odds 47
Newfoundland Standard Time 48
The Arches 49
Now Is Not the Time 50
Lust for Life 51
Recurring Dream 52
We Could Fill a River 53
Weight 55
Gerald Douglas Walbourne 56

Card 58
Tuckamore 59
Dysregulation 60
Retrofit 62
I Didn't Just Let This Happen 63
Kuntew 64
Bastard 65
I Didn't Just Let This Happen 66
I Still Dream of Moose 67
Self-Doubt as Harvey Keitel as the Wolf 68
First Date 69
How Do I Say This? 70
Acknowledgements and Thanks 73
Notes 75

Another Visit from My Grandfather

This time, the dream's outdoors.
Not the usual backdrop of his bedroom
in Dunfield Park. We're now in a field
of high grass, a rolling bog surrounding
one of our favourite ponds.

We sit on plain wooden chairs. Our weight,
though, doesn't push their legs through
the ground with a squelch. The grass stutters
on and off, glitching, reminds me — my time
with him is fleeting, always has been.

A stream idles by, pulls off a trick
only running water can — embodying
both permanence and flux at once.
The brash squawks of blue jays scrape
the air with their impatience, while
a chest-puffed grey jay pitches
on my arm, expects scraps of bread.

This time, his grey hair's white, mixed
with sprigs of pale green Spanish moss,
his sunken cheeks stubbled with patches
of lichen. Save for his gold canine, his teeth
are polished black granite, quartz flecks
glinting as he greets me in my father's voice.

He surveys the pond, the flickering
grass we're surrounded by, but no sound
escapes his lips. His eyes go near black,
an autumnal midnight blue without moon
or stars, and he turns to me, looks me full on,
laughs my own laugh and assures me

don't worry, you'll understand it all soon enough.

Guilt

At twenty-one, he chose to commit to her,
become a father to a toddler when he was just
a kid himself. Year after year he left the island
for work, months away in tobacco fields,
in factories, suiting up for asbestos removal,
tar sands and offshore oil. Long before direct
deposit, he'd bring home a stack of uncashed
cheques in a rubber-banded envelope, hand
them to her, and say, *Let's do this*.

But I couldn't ask Dad about the man-shaped
hole in my past, who walked out before I was
born, who couldn't be arsed to pay child support.
I was a walking question mark, not allowed
to ask why I wasn't good enough, what I'd
done wrong. Dad was scared I'd want to go
live with the stranger. I didn't know why
I felt shame for wanting to know the truth.

My mother, caught between her husband
and son, sometimes sat me down, gave me
details. His name, that I had another set
of grandparents, that my mystery grandfather
once came to see me, but his wife detested
mom for ruining a young man's life.

Mom's crowd was harsh, too. No place
for bastards in a small-town pastor's family.
I'm not sure what was said, what realizations
happened, but room was made for me, eventually.
I became so close with mom's parents that I spent
every Saturday night with them for years.

We'd rent a Nintendo, pick up bags of chips,
a bottle of Coke. Sunday school the next morning,
until I aged out and sat in the pews, surrounded
by raptured adults singing praise to the same force
that tried weighing my mother down with shame.
I abandoned church at twelve, haven't looked back.

What do I do with this lived story?
With these people whose love for me
was twisted up in fear, faith, and shame?
Tell me, what would you do?

Corner Brook

> The company maintained considerable informal influence over municipal affairs after amalgamation, and many of the residents of Townsite preferred company paternalism over local democracy. Similar to the ways colonial powers' relationships with the colonized carried influence into the post-colonial age, complex and flexible corporate hegemony in Corner Brook echoed through the post-company era.
>
> — Neil White, *Company Towns: Corporate Order and Community*

A town full of trees, so much summer canopy
you can barely see the roofs from Three Bear
Mountain. Come fall, sugar maples burn bright
orange and red, birch's sunlight-yellow shining
through the shorter, damper days. It's not a stretch
to walk West Street, caught up in a half-dozen
chats with people you know by first name.
Some days, that feeling's enough to carry you.

I love my hometown, but it's hard-won
and wavers in the face of our history —
a town built on divisions of class and race,
not yet five generations old. I still hear things
like, *The Mi'kmaq should go back to Nova*
Scotia, I'm not spending my taxes on 'em.
I still have to walk away, shame and anger
twisting in my guts, when someone accuses
one of us of *sucking on the Aboriginal funding*
teat. When I see a young couple and toddler,
one parent remarking to the other, *He walks*
so slow 'cause he's got your Jackytar blood.

You may think I'm being over-sensitive, but
I know this town. I've spent years steaming

your lattes, mowing your lawns, laying sod
to kill the dandelions you hated the sight of,
worked in your Zellers, dollar stores, produced
and hosted your arts events, worked at Grenfell
Art Gallery, read to your toddlers at the library,
sold you hot dogs from a cart on Broadway.

I've been treated differently as writer vs. labourer
vs. government employee. I've seen your surprise
in finding out I'm educated, published, *and* grew up
in public housing. Oh, I know. Hometowns are like this.
They make you feel so embraced, so known and loved,
yet always reminding you of your place. I love you,
Corner Brook, but now I want to love me, too.

This All Happened?

> Most of us think that history is the past. It's not.
> History is the stories we tell about the past.
> — Thomas King

i) relative perception

Back in Toronto, the same place my mother
left Corner Brook for. I'm just a year old,
oblivious to the friction I'd caused by being born.
We're in the Caribou Club, where Harry Hibbs
packs the house with homesick Newfoundlanders,
where my grandfather plays open-mic nights.
Back when my grandparents still smoked, drank
rum 'n' Cokes. Long before prayer and small-town
talk steered him to become a Pentecostal pastor.

The bar's also their living room, every table
set up comfortably with a couch and wingback
chair on repeat. Each setting displaying a large
Bible, its zippered closure undone, splayed offering
of gold-gilt pages, Christ's words under neon red.
My grandparents, mother, and me somehow sitting
at all the tables at once. Pop's accordion a remote
for the "multicordion" — in lieu of a jukebox
he'd built a case full of glowing glass-tube amps,
bellows, pneumatic hoses. A hoarded lifetime
of tithings in saved change lining the bottom.

Each note played would brighten the lights,
flush rushes of air through the hoses, bring
his voice over the speakers blowing benediction
as he whipped the accordion around his wrists,
left then right, slinging it behind his back, eyes
shut in ecstasy, my grandmother's hands thrown
up in rapture while my mother smoked, lit each

one from the last, unimpressed. My grandfather's
eyes go wide, he speaks in Christ's voice,
quoting Hank Williams — *If you're gonna sing,*
sing 'em somethin' they can understand.

My grandmother, cross-stitching in scrolls,
her perfect up-do catching sheens of light from
every table, asks my mother — *Can my grandson*
read music? Slow snakes of smoke from my mother's
nose as she shakes her head *no.* Her mother shrugs,
there are other ways to serve. Mom musses my hair,
her eyes' green glint, keen as a cat, her smile
a drawer of knives — *not the worst thing I've done.*

I'm in the room, can hear their words, the music,
smell tobacco smoke and sour beer, but my hand
passes through her shoulder when I try to say,
Look at us, you did damn well. I see my infant self
in a bassinet look back at me with a shrug. I realize
this isn't the way it happened, nor is it a fiction.
The accordion hits the floor, its black and white
pearl keys fall out like old teeth, the lights come up.
I'm no longer in the Caribou Club. No more music,
just a gentle lapping of water against stone.

ii) status

I'm waist-deep in Parson's Pond, my mother's parents
in the water with me. Instead of baptizing me in Jesus's
name, my grandfather falls gently backward. A small kick
from his legs, he asks, *Sure, I can lead you beside quiet waters,*
but let's just go for a swim? Nan, all grace and sunglasses,
floats by with a crossword, nonchalantly asks, *Six-letter word*
for social rank, *starts and ends with* s*?*

My father's folks paddle past, the phrase *Teach 'em to fish*
runs the length of their canoe. They raise their mugs
of tea with a wink as they tow the sun across the sky,
their grins possess a knowing I can't quite place. I don't realize
I'm floating on my back until the moon appears above me
and the pond's gently in my ears, whispering, *As above,*
so below in the voices of both grandmothers at once.

My father scoops me up, *You're a little lost, but*
that's nothin' a few hours around the fire won't fix.
He stands full height, stars caught in his beard, carries
me home in strides, boots brushing tips of black spruce
like grass. From up here, we can see Sandy Point, can see
St. Paul Island as he wades out the bay, *Elmastukwek*
suddenly on my lips as we head to Cedar Cove.

He takes my wallet, with its government-issued cards,
takes my Christian guilt and self-doubt, drops them
into an old coffee-can kettle. I ask, *Why can't I just burn it all?*
He hands me some matches, nods behind me. My mother
steps in from the surf on a wave of rolling capelin — *some things*
we shed, some we're steeped in. She adds the rising tide,
a few newspaper obituaries, the open throat of a pitcher plant.

Together, we build a pyre of kindling and driftwood, fill
it with birchbark, but I want to run. She hands me the kettle,
kisses my cheek. *We know who you are, but we can't make*

you believe it. Shaking, I strike a match to watch the bark recoil, gift itself to fire. Not brave, just tired of telling myself the same story, I spit the phrase *not enough* into the can, break into heaves and sobs, let the kettle boil.

I Didn't Just Let This Happen

I'm afraid of you punching me. Afraid of your stalk and snarl as you circle me, laughing, daring me to hit you back, knowing I won't.

You outsize me and your violence confuses me. I am too naïve, too sensitive.

We're friends. Our parents are neighbours, also friends. Yet I can't remember a day over the last several years when I didn't wish we'd never met. Sometimes I let my mind wander and find myself wishing at least one of us dead.

Your fist connects with my small frame, but I've gotten used to it. A bruise that, now, I can't recall ever not having.

C'mon! Hit me back, what the fuck's wrong with you? A dare I can't accept. You spit at my feet, I'm thankful it's not in my face. You light two cigarettes, hand me one without a word.

I Visit Margie with Moose Meat

for Margie Benoit-Wheeler

I brought Margie two bottles of moose,
a thank-you visit as I left town for K'jipuktuk.
When Corner Brook finally acknowledged
Crow Gulch with a Mi'kmaw-made mural,
an opening ceremony complete with ribbon,
I knew my grandparents were there, nodding
with thanks at Margie, who minced no words
when she took to the mic, told of how this town
looked down on her community, our people.

After the ceremony, when the news crews
and politicians were long gone, Margie
gifted me a memory from when she was
young. She'd watched Ella and Rudy walk
the tracks back from town, just married.
Nan's makeshift veil flowing behind them
as they walked into the rest of their lives,
started writing the story I'd one day find
myself inheriting, trying to live up to.

Before I stood to leave, she put up a finger
and left the kitchen. Came back with a hand-
made necklace, blue and white beads, black
cord, a bear claw exclaiming itself at the centre.
My colonized mind raced to *Am I allowed
to wear this?* but Margie's face told me all
I needed to know. Something older, bigger
than both of us was at work here.

Childhood Photo

Grainy. Faded greens of black spruce
in the background. Alders and fireweed,
the odd past-flower coltsfoot dotting
the foreground. Ghosts of birch and fir
like matchsticks strewn among cutover
throughout. We're thirty clicks in back
of Logger School Road, a day of trouting
at a pond we don't tell most people about.

Dad's wearing a plaid jacket, faded jeans,
the full beard I haven't seen in years.
His eyes are squinted, the sort-of-formal
expression of one not used to photos.
I'm in a striped polo shirt, the word *LOVE*
shouting itself from my ball cap, tan pants,
no idea what to do with my hands.

I'm five, he's just twenty-four. His right
arm is bent, hand hanging loose, unsure
of the appropriate father-son pose. His left
hand rests on my head, claims me as his son,
but we're yet to really grow into our bond —
highly sensitive, picky eater and world-on-
his-shoulders stoic meeting each other halfway.

I'm forty-one this year, he's sixty. Seeing
his hair slowly grey while my beard does
the same, I'm finally realizing how young
we were. I wish I'd leaned into his leg, kept
my eyes on the camera and whispered,
just to him, *Don't worry, we've got this.*

I Didn't Just Let This Happen

You and ______ are making out in the corner of the camp we built from stolen plywood. *What the fuck is he doin' here?* she keeps asking. You keep telling her I'm watching the door, not to worry about it. I add that I'm fine to wait outside, to go home out of it, to which you growl, *You sit the fuck there and don't move.* In a moment of pleading apology I catch her eye, but she just gives me the finger.

You, thinking this hilarious, tell her to do it again, but this time even she finds it all a bit too much. She shoves you aside and lights a smoke, asks again what the fuck I'm doing here. I tell her, *I don't really know,* and she leaves, struts down the trail shouting something about not being anyone's bitch.

The Waves

Cedar Cove, but not quite. Parking lots
full of sedans, mostly nondescript American
models, the odd Volkswagen or Sonata.
Rentals. The interpretation centre is a glass
and steel-beamed insult to a lighthouse, a sign
over the door neon-tubing itself at me in flashes.
Essentially, a gas station minus the pumps—
rolling hot dogs, Bic lighters with team logos,
seventeen ways to charge your phone.

Visitors are encouraged to roam the beach,
gather flotsam and jetsam and arrange
it in block capitals to spell *HELP* across
the rocks. The first to do so wins an all-inclusive
week's stay on the Hibernia oil platform, which
they could then upgrade from the labourer's package
to foreman's so they wouldn't have to work fourteen
weeks just to afford to go home.

The lowest deck of the centre is the Fluvarium,
as advertised on signs along the crumbling
two-lane road that led me here, among billboards
for long-gone cafés and four-star inns, an abandoned
copper mine, and struggling salmon rivers.

Didactic panels explain the parallels
between this island's love for a boom/bust
economy and our historic ties to the sea.
The waves are microcosm for the tides,
tides are metaphor for change, but only
change that returns, predictably, to status quo.

The panel ends with *Britannica*'s definition
of a wave—*A propagation of disturbances from place*

to place in a regular and organized way— then ends with the question, *Which wave do you prefer? The one approaching or the one receding?* Under the text, a decal reminds me that the premises are monitored by video. The security company's logo in red on a peeling sticker laid over a blue one in the exact same shape.

Ten Percent

> It's taken them 10,000 years to get here, but you can
> discover them in just a click.
> — newfoundlandandlabrador.com

Ten-thousand-year-old files citing the last time
earth could breathe easy. They break off and coast
slowly toward oblivion, mounted by fools posing
for photos, crack-shot to pieces to make vodka, brew
blue-bottled beer. A North Atlantic wind tries to bite
through a dozen bright, overpriced, windproof jackets.
Some purchased just for this trip, to end up in Value
Village, left in the Airbnb, to the crew in lieu of a tip.

This last decade has been great for business.
Bigger bergs and more of them, people flying in
to be seen seeing their first. No one wants to ruin
the mood by saying something stupid about climate,
superstitious it'll somehow bring in the feds to shut
it down. We know no one actually wants to send
the captain and crew back to the oil sands, the Labrador
mines, to Service Canada to stake another forty-four-week
claim. So let's get back to this boat, these well-meaning
tourists, operators, and the entrepreneurial spirit, this annual
dance with Employment Insurance. It's an honest living,
a tangle of privilege and glacial melt. We're all in bed together,
hard to say whose foot that is, whose ass is most exposed.

What will we do when it all comes to an end?
Get our stamps for next year's claim as we cash in
on watching the North Pole drift past Bonavista?
Maybe we'll savour that last flash of brilliant white
clashing with the Hawaiian shirts of Mr. and Mrs.
Claus, cold drinks in their hands, reindeer on the grill,
Prince's *1999* blaring from a Bluetooth speaker.
Finally taking that vacation they always talked about.

Steep Steps toward Home

Sun. Sun laminated onto snow
and sealed by wind. Hardcover.
Before this, though, knee-deep
slog through soft stuff. The heart
jumps into the ears, a pulse
in the eyelids begging *no more,*
no more as the throat sores
from so much laboured breath.

Back to sun. Back to leaning
into the steep of this hill. Wind
tries to keep you down, gravity
tries to keep you down. Aching
knees and back and bones trying
to keep you down. A body defied
by its driver, by a mind's stubborn
fix, *do not fail.* Wondering if
there's any virtue in dying while
doing what you love.

Agh, enough! Enough of this
self-punishment, enough tough talk
of rock and wind, so much effort
just to hide in plain sight. I can't
seem to cry so I'm hiking my guts
out until something in me gives.

Then, I reach the top. So close
to Guernsey Island I could walk out
across air, brush off the snow and sit.
Legs kicking out over the gulf, I blow
a kiss to the Magdalens, peer around
Anticosti to catch a glimpse of gulls
in Gaspé Bay. Lazy, in love with being

alone up here, I yawn, stretch my arms,
barely notice when I prick my finger
on Long Point.

I notice that my windproof coat
is the same colour as the ocean,
as the sky, as all the things we never
said when we should have. All this
inexhaustible blue wears me down.

I'm gasping as the wind whips against
my body, whips me until I break
into heaves and sobs — I'm somehow
in the driver's seat, engine running,
heat on bust, drying salt and snot against
my skin. Dumb with grief, mumbling
we tried, we tried, into the hot,
thick emptiness of a rental car.

I Didn't Just Let This Happen

We're trouting, sitting on a beaver dam with a few sandwiches, a couple spliffs. We've had a good run today. Must be four hours now, and no sign of violence.

This all stops when I land three trout in a row and you aren't getting any bites. I offer to switch spots, let you cast where I was having luck, but you're having none of it. You walk back to the quad, start it and rip away on two wheels. You pass back and forth a few times, once going so far that I can't hear you anymore. No idea if you're going to leave me to walk back.

You finally return, shit-eating grin pasted across your face. Satisfied by the velocity, the noise, the embodied aggression of an engine. *How many trout we get,* you ask. I count the fish out loud, just over a dozen. You toss me your pocket knife and say, *You know what to do.*

I squat on the shore, legs folded underneath me, cleaning the trout, tossing the heads and guts into deeper water for the eels. You stand full height, clearing your throat and your nose in disgust, each glob of spit smacking the back of my shirt with a wet cotton thud.

Or Perhaps You Have

Still dark. We sit silent in the truck.
The ticks of the cooling engine mix
with the Land's yawn and pre-dawn
stretch. A proper September chill
reminds me how short our summers
really are, how much good can come
from a Thermos of coffee.

Our ears become keen enough to hear
a nearby stream find its way back to
a pond we can't yet see, enough to hear
the forest floor yield to the feet of spruce
grouse, pine marten, falling bits of seeds
and cones from the mouths of squirrels.

Blue-black gives way to grey
as daylight creeps over the edge
of the continent, reaches this island
half an hour before the rest of Turtle
Island, rouses the dark mass of antler
bone and fur from its grassy bed, watches
as our accidental mascot's spindle-thin
legs trot its brown bulk out onto bog.

How to step into this lineage, to write
about an animal integral to this island's
identity, yet so alien it had to be introduced
twice. To write this is to graft breath
and marrow to pure rock and recognize
this bond as real love, as more than just
good enough, to accept this come-from-away
as family, as lover, as one of our own.

Back to the bog — my mother takes
a deep breath, raises the iron sight
to the spot just behind the front leg,
those first few ribs encasing the lungs,
everything vital. Knowing that to take
this life to feed your own is still an act
of love, reverence. An act filled with the risk
of getting it wrong, of missing the point,
missing the shot. The weighted responsibility
of enacting this death with a good heart —
the soft bog cradles the animal to rest.

Maybe you've never seen so much
blood, felt the heat of a living thing
radiate from itself to thaw your numbed
fingers, or perhaps you have, and you're
as lost for the right words as I am, fumbling
to relay such immediacy, such connection,
as its energy slowly transfers, pure intimacy,
from its earthly form into yours.

My Uncouth Mouth

> We learned that our accents were wrong and that we ought to leave our strange expressions at home.
> — Mary Dalton

i) Aurora, Ontario, July 2000

My first week of factory work.
Still a boy, seventeen, promised
a couch, a ride from Newfoundland
to Newmarket. Had a hundred bucks,
two packs of smokes. Encouraged
by my folks to move out, grow up.

The coffee truck pulled up, my eyes
widened to see all manner of snacks,
hot coffee, three brands of cigs, cooler
full of bottled water, Pepsi, and Gatorade.
I stood there gawking, unable to choose.

New guy, eh? I got hot food, cold
drinks, SUNshine Girls, all on credit
if you need it. I needed it, having
spent my hundred bucks on work
boots, half a pack of smokes left.
Thanks! Can I get a can of drink,
a pack of Players, and a sandwich?

A can of drink? Jesus H. Christ,
another Newfie. It's a tin of pop, guy.
No one's gonna take you seriously
if you don't speak right.

ii) Kelowna, British Columbia, March 2017

Standing at a cash register, retail
small talk greasing the transaction —

Where're you from?

Newfoundland, moved here for school.

Oh! I love Newfies! I invite them
to all my parties, they all talk so funny —
people love it!

Gut-punched, trying to temper
this indignation with a semblance
of empathy for this ignorance,
my mouth opens and I find my feet —

We're not parrots, we're not party
favours. I'll take my receipt.

On the bus home, my chest thrums
with shame but I can't tell if I feel
it for being a Newfoundlander or
for having been rude to someone
who, I'm guessing, meant no real
harm. Years later, I still don't know.

iii) Banff Centre for the Arts, Alberta, February 2016

Walking into the bistro, greeted
by its glass-walled, snow-peaked
mountain view, it's hard not to think,
Bond villain, hard to ignore the stone
wall carved with donor names, dollar
amounts exceeding what I'll make
in a decade. Hard to feel comfortable.

I've been advised to introduce myself
to a well-known figure in this scene,
so I get a drink, walk over, say hello.
You're from Newfoundland, yeah?
I nod, sipping. Then, the slight rise
in volume, the jaunty body movement,
sudden smile of expecting a joke to land—
Bet you're damn proud of it too, huh?!

Like you, right now, were I to simply
read these words, I might dismiss them.
If you were there, though, if you've ever
felt that nagging, subtle expectation
to *yes, sir* your way through a conversation,
you know the assumptions made about you
before you even walk into a room.

I wish I'd said, *Yes, but only when I'm not
being shamed for being proud.* Instead, I nod
into my drink. Answer some stock questions
about moose, if I've ever been to George Street.

I Visit My Grandfather with Sea Trout

The year before he died, I brought him
four thick sea-run trout. Caught them
off the point in Brake's Cove, biked back
into town against the sunset, squinting.
No idea how lucky I was to be young.

I knocked on his door, walked in. He stood
at the kitchen window, mug of tea in hand,
staring. Most likely missing my grandmother.
I opened my pack, took out the Sobeys bag
sagging with the weight of the fish.

He took the bag, eyes wide as he hefted
it up and down, puffing me up. Cleaned
the biggest one first, the belly giving up
its guts as his thumb scraped the spine,
plopped the offal back into the plastic bag.

It's one of my favourite memories.
This rare moment when I hoped I'd proved
I was more than a picky eater, more than
that *emotional* kid married into the family.
Too bad, though, I also missed the point.

What a perfect chance to have asked him
for a cup of tea while I cleaned the trout,
placed the bodies in a bowl of salt water,
put them in the fridge. Boiled the kettle
again and sat with him at the table.

A chance to ask about *his* Crow Gulch,
if he ever heard Nan speak Mi'kmaw.
Ask how he met the love of his life.
I biked home in the growing dusk, blind
to the reciprocity I'd denied us both.

I Didn't Just Let This Happen

First year of high school. I'm hanging out with a group from West Side, one of whom I've been close with since elementary school. I figure this a safe enough bet, as there's a grade 11 in the group, too. After a few weeks of nervously settling into a group and a routine, the same table at lunch, things shift.

One Monday, at lunch time, I meet up with the b'ys in the cafeteria, sit down and take out my lunch: RC Cola, snack cake, and a sandwich. Lather, rinse, repeat. Grade 11 looks at me, his brow lowered, the sorta look that levels you if you can't return it immediately. Pristine intimidation. Pristine. I, all of 5'5" and 140 lbs., wilt accordingly.

Lemme see your lunch.

. . .

Don't make me ask again. Gimme your lunch.

I see what's happening, paralyzed by a fear already well established. I watch myself hand over my lunch, some out-of-body moment I know I'll regret forever but cannot stop.

How many smokes you have?

I silently remove the cassette case from my jacket pocket, show him the four cigarettes I have for the day, the ones I bought from my buddy at the bus stop this morning.

Half, now.

I watch myself comply. This sets a precedent that carries through the entirety of grade 10. And gets worse.

Canada's Happy Province

My heart is breaking for Mud Lake,
for the northern cod, the white pine,
for twice-fractured Qalipu families,
for the woodland caribou, the Beothuk,
the great auk, for every cashier robbed
at ______-point, for those who end up
in corner stores, throwing gas on a trainee's
uniform then striking a match, demanding
enough cash to get through the week—

all the breath in a room, held.

My heart is breaking and all I can offer
is living metaphor, lifting moose bone
and brook trout to the light, hoping
you see, in one hand, this coarse-haired
beauty etched into my skull, the other hand
offering this fleeting thing, its speckled flesh
flickering like a night sky of stars, wishing
I had answers, or actions, something less
useless than poetry to lay at your feet.

Safety

In the back of my grandparents'
car, on the way home from church,
I'd sit quietly in some itchy, hand-
me-down Sunday best. My tiny chest
wound tight, counting streetlights,
I'd keep an eye out for the corner store
I knew meant a left turn into the heart
of Dunfield Park. Coming home.

Until I saw the Pepsi and Du Maurier
logos of the store's marquee, until we passed
the tree-named side streets — Alder, Beech,
Cedar, Dogwood, Elm, and Fir — I'd sit
convinced that I'd be driven past the store,
the car wouldn't turn left, and I'd be dropped
off at some stranger's place. Given away.

Housewarming

I show up early, quickly tasked with hanging
Star Wars paper cut-outs like folded snowflakes.
Reassured they've got the food covered, I slowly
separate stormtroopers, delicate Death Stars,
X-wings and Yodas, some nondescript Jedi.

A host calls me over, shows me some caribou
tufting they're working on. My grandfather's face
comes to mind — how his eyes would be wide,
gold canine catching light, how he'd ask as much
about the work of the hunt as the work of art.

Before I can excuse myself, tears. Choking
on how much I miss him, that he'll never see
how much I love him. I can't tell you how long
I stood there, grief-struck, wishing I could press
the tufted fur to my face, feel closer to him.

The Believer's Daily Planner: July 23, 1989–July 22, 1990

My mother's parents were Pentecostal. Not quite
the speaking-in-tongues sort, but strict enough
to warrant the old joke about premarital sex leading
to dancing. He was a pastor; Nan was a missionary,
as was his second wife, whom we called Aunt Marie.
In the last months of her short life, Marion told Pop
and Marie to make each other happy after she died
and meant it. Any way I look at it, this level of grace
transcends religion, defies any egoic logic I can muster.

In the '80s, Marion and Gerald built churches
in Hopedale. She wore beaded sealskin, he gave
sermons in Inuktitut. In the 2000s, he and Marie
lived in a trailer in Natuashish, made breakfast
for school kids. As a Newfoundland Mi'kmaw,
this missionary half of my past is hard to sit with.
They were kind to me, but how does kindness
manifest through a Christian lens? I'm tired of
trying to reconcile mistrust and love.

He left me a book. A diary written to me while Marion
got her first liver transplant. The cover is fake leather,
The Believer's Daily Planner embossed across the front
in gold. Inside, a stock message of faith from Jimmy
Swaggart himself. A book hard not to judge by its cover.
Pop wrote to me every day for a year, documenting
what began as daily life in northern Labrador then quickly
turned to flights to Goose Bay, Corner Brook, then Halifax,
chasing medical care as Nan's body turned against her.

I can't tell if this book works to cement or undo my self-doubt.
The first Indigenous language I heard was Inuktitut, filtered
through my grandfather's Christian mouth. The first Indigenous

clothing I saw was the sealskin snowsuit my nan wore home
during a winter visit to Newfoundland. I would bury my face
in fur, the deep smell of seal mixing with chopped syllables,
my head flooded with questions I'd take decades to articulate.
They brought my parents a caribou hide, so unlike the dark,
coarse moose I was used to, no idea that caribou were here first.

Herd

Another dream. Not recurring,
but I wish it was. Avalon, a barren
dotted with legs, and legs, and legs.

Thousands of caribou, grazing under
a half-mauzy day of sun and showers,
not a single head raised at my approach.

At first, I mistook the blunt thump
in my skull for my own pulse, but
it was interrupted — no, interspersed

with huffs and snorts, the soft yield
of grass and sedge to tooth and rough
tongue, the scrape of lichen from stone.

I'd like to say I walked, naked and sure,
into their midst, all antlers and wet, black
eyes. I wish their gentle, barrelled bodies

had slowly parted as I walked, that I sat
in their centre unhindered, and came
to some sort of rude understanding.

But I knew little of their countless
unsheltered winters, how they've been
ousted by moose as the island's mascot.

I tried to push myself through their living
thicket of hoof and shed velvet, convinced
I'd found their middle, but was squeezed

out the other side. I stood at the herd's edge,
trying to listen. Gutted by the ache to belong.

I Didn't Just Let This Happen

A few months into the school year, the threat of winter in the morning air. We're outside in our usual huddle, one among dozens of huddles wafting tobacco smoke. I haven't seen Grade 11 yet this morning, pretending that his absence doesn't heighten my anxiety.

My parents bought me a name-brand jacket, a windbreaker with three stripes and a logo. I'm proud of it, no doubt. All those years of knock-offs and hand-me-downs, cut-off shorts. I love this jacket but I'm trying to play it cool. It's just as well—I feel a pressure on my shoulder, then the heat of a lit cigarette on my skin. He walks away, looks back with a sneer and laughs, *Nice jacket.*

Attention

Consider the brook trout. Its body
banded with aurora, flecked with stars,
the white comet tails of its fin tips
cutting the current like lace.

Its exquisite hinge of lips, ready
to nip black flies — a moment
between worlds, a small swirl
on the surface like a flash of galaxy.

Now, consider the universe. Or, if
it feels easier, local, the Milky Way.
We've named the nebulae, have finally
seen the fish eye of a black hole.

Consider the hidden gems of spawn,
each orange egg a brilliant sun. Its gills
are solar flares of blood, its swim bladder
an otherworldly stolen breath.

We keep casting satellites into orbit,
playing catch 'n' release with the billions
of texts we send each other, daily.
I contemplate all this from the canoe.

Rod tucked under my arm, I'm landing
a large trout. Its body bucking to break
free, reminding me of its urge to fill
its own sky with shooting stars of fry.

The hook removed, I cradle the fish
for one last look, unable to remember
the last time I paid so much attention
to something other than myself.

At Odds

The envelope nestles between wool
socks, not sealed but the flap folded in.
Three months' rent stashed, the first smart
thing I've done in years. The slim stack
of twenties has my number, though. Calls
lovingly, knows my craving. I watch myself
pull back the flap, remove a single bill, slide
it into my pocket. Harmless. I open my coat,
fold the envelope in half before cramming
it down an inside pocket with a sigh.

Casual Jack's, a quiet Tuesday, bartender
playing Power Keno. I wait out their hand,
order a shot, a pint, pack of smokes. Leave
a twenty as tip, take the machine farthest back,
my eye on the door. I reach for the envelope,
feed in forty bucks, then sixty, another sixty.
Max bet. Lose it all on purpose. I pull my hat
lower over my face, lose a hundred more.

More shots, more pints, ashtray past full,
bile burning my throat. Not from the drink,
not the hangover I know I'm owed, but because
I'll have to face my mother, have to admit
that I love myself so little that I'm compelled
to do the right thing just long enough
to underline my longing to fall from a height.

Newfoundland Standard Time

*Screen capture from my iPhone, June 21, 2021

The Arches

Driving back down the coast, now. Gunned
for St. Anthony two days ago, chasing icebergs.
Missed the big one by a week. Sea and sky seem
to meet, but look closer, squint. They never marry,
horizon is engagement made indefinite. Staring
at Labrador's southern shore, forcing small talk
about weather, how the car won't heat up.
Kidding ourselves, *We'll try again next year.*

All weekend I couldn't tell up from down.
You'd hit the tent hours early, hardly a word
between us. I stood on the beach, numb, slamming
cans of Keith's. The few stray bergs left broke up
overnight. Pretending to sleep, we keened our ears
as each piece cracked like rifle shot, splinter and slow
splash as the ice righted itself, resurfaced.

At the Arches we stop, stretch our legs.
For a moment, we watch waves gnawing rock.
Your thick green sweater breaks my heart
as I lean on the car, watch you comb the beach
for nothing in particular.

Now Is Not the Time

The selfie was no longer our go-to display
of beauty. Now, smartphone cameras scanned
not for aesthetic value, but for the weight of our
hearts, our interactions with the world. The same
technology that produced lab-grown meat could
replicate intricate suits of flowers so complex
and delicate they fit the body like skin.

Initially, social media was on board. The skins
trended on Twitter while TikTok tried making
its own filter, but the algorithms kept missing
the point. This was a measure of how we'd lived,
not how we looked, expressed in photosynthesis.
We had no control over what flowers we'd get —
to engage with the process was to trust it.

Your flowers were deep blue, they shimmered
to purple and back, the centres bright yellow.
You said you'd never felt more yourself, blushed
a flash of poppies when our eyes met. You asked
me to join you, finding myself head-to-toe in forget-
me-nots with undulating waves of midnight blue.

We stood, shimmered together for a moment,
your blooms slowly tracking the sun, mine still
humming in deliberation. My irises turned
marigold, followed the curve of your shoulder
as its petals tasted a change in the air. You turned,
brushed a blade of grass from my cheek, and said,
Now is not the time to fear the bees.

Lust for Life

Iggy Pop got a job in the cemetery
across the bay from Corner Brook,
the one my father worked at one summer,
the one all my dead family and friends
live in. Iggy said he'd never met him,
but heard good things about my old man.
To make sure I said hello from him.

We talked about flowers, Iggy's love
of carnations and peonies, the unsung
virtues of dandelions. He refused to
elaborate on his thoughts of the plastic
flowers flanking the odd headstone,
but said he liked the pick and shovel
of the job, the heavy peace of death,
earth, and polished stone.

He patted some black turf around
the stems of some poppies, their heads
drooping and bobbing in the wind,
the flesh of his own body sagging, but
what an articulate manner of speech
when he pushed his hair out of his face,
sized me up full on, and asked, *Why is it*
so many of your friends chose to be here?

Recurring Dream

TCH, driving through Gros Morne.
I put my foot down, then down again,
passing everything for sport. Engine
kicks back as I white-knuckle the wheel,
teeth gnashed, tempting the inevitable.

Two moose rush the pavement, the car
becomes ATV. Thigh-thick spruce
and birch smashed off, then the ugly
crunch of metal and bone, followed by
the smell of talc and gasoline.

We Could Fill a River

The Wolastoq flows below me. Spring
ice is receding, this year's first blue herons
bring sun. They call me outside to warm
my snow-weary bones. I've crossed this bridge
often, stopped to watch people fish, couldn't
resist comparing this river to the rum-brown
water of the Maqtukwek I've never fished
but grew up convinced I'd drown in.

I'd watched *The Country*, broke down
with bucking shoulders, my body taking
the pain as I realized how deep the mistrust
went. Began to understand how a story could
make me feel unwelcome in my own hometown.

I needed to see Qalipu through both eyes.
One fixed on my own experience, the other
with openness to five decades of Flat Bay's
pain. Of Stephenville's and the Crossing's,
of St. George's and Shallop Cove's pain.
The more I saw, the more room I made
for truths other than mine. I had to call you,
no matter how scared I was of breaking
protocol with my ignorance.

Two years after I watched *The Country*,
I crossed that bridge. Drew in a deep breath.
I'd had your number for a few days, afraid
to call, to admit that I had no idea who I was,
ashamed of my lack of blood quantum, being
adopted, that I couldn't yet speak Mi'kmaw.
That we could fill a river with all I didn't know.

I'd never spoken with an Elder before, but
it wasn't long before our laughter dissolved
my anxiety and you reminded me — *You're one*
of thousands on the island going through this.
I walked back across the bridge. The adage of never
stepping in the same river twice crossed my mind,
but I knew the Wolastoq hadn't changed. Land never
needs to. The work was always mine to do.

Weight

Age-old grease gone sour. The air dense
with Varsol, sweat, noise. Herculean clunk
of steel punched through by 750 tons of machine
begetting machine on loop. Think density,
a heaviness born from dying stars.

He worked the punch press. Shaved head,
shit-eating grin. Loved firing up the forklift,
laying rubber on the shop floor, madman's
laughter mixed with smoke.

Fridays, he'd wait till the boss knocked off
and walk to his car, drag in a bag of clubs,
a dozen golf balls. Spend the afternoon trying
to hit the GO Train as it passed behind the shop.

That scream froze our blood. 600-lb. steel
beam, the pressure ruptured his fingertips.
Flesh and fat escaped skin, his tendons and knuckles
rendered useless, as bone gave way to the bullied
reality of physics. Vomit splashed his steel toes,
splashed our coveralls as we failed to free him.

Afterward, he just sat there. Shaking. Cigarette
burning absent-minded in his left hand; the right
half wrapped in his Guns N' Roses T-shirt. Pissed
off about missing work, embarrassed for crying
in front of us. Asked quietly for a ride to the hospital.

Signed the triage nurse's forms
with a series of awkward *X*'s.

Gerald Douglas Walbourne

ICU, August. First a stroke, now
a coma. My grandfather the pastor,
the superhero, finite symbol of infinite
good, lies fetal, fed by tubes.

One for food, another in his nose
for air, one hidden under his gown,
leaking yellow-brown and shedding
light on what we spend our entire lives
wiping away, flushing, embarrassed.

One leg and one arm lying limp, burdening
the other side as it twitches under his
dead-life mass. His good hand is tethered
to the bed with a knotted bedsheet so he
doesn't yank out the tubes before their time.

Aunt Lisa, my mother's only sister,
is vigilant. She wipes away the coffee-
coloured stuff his shallow breaths bring
to the surface. Nurses come and go.

Uncle Gerry (Gerald Jr.) argues with
doctors, armed with faith and the shock
of loss, he wears out words like *miracle,*
second opinion, CAT scan.

Uncle Trevor, blue-eyed baby of the family,
finds himself angry with God despite his
own faith. He's still sore from losing his mother
a dozen years ago. I can only concur.

My mother, black sheep, the smoker who
went rogue, whose faith was placed in love

beyond the church, remains strong. Bleary-
eyed and clutching a ragged Kleenex,
she's the one bearing bad news to our distant
family. Phone to her ear, her tears wiped
away as each call repeats the grim details.

Aunt Marie. Not really an aunt but words
like *step-grandmother* and *second wife*
lack the love she shared with him. With all
of us. She sits, beside herself, talking to him
as if he's not in the next room, strapped
to his deathbed as his tethered hand squeezes
and releases the white sheet. Dying.

My grandfather will be her second husband
lost to a stroke. I try but can't even face her.
Shame slaps me across the face, kicks my guts
in, and I know it's time to tell him goodbye.

For a while, I just stand there. Watching.
The only time I've ever seen him scared,
and he'll never even know. Taking his hand,
I'm amazed — there's an old photo of us,
I'm months old, asleep on his chest. So small.
His hands were like hammers, yet so tender
toward me, larval in my yellow sleeper.

Now, his wedding band is slack against his finger
and I'd give anything to scoop him up, carry him
out of here. Bring him to the island in Rocky Pond
where he camped for entire summers with Nan,
let him lie on my chest, quietly slip away.

Card

The day it arrived, I held the envelope
in my hand, trembling and too anxious
to open it. My father and sister already
had their cards, neither of them had any
doubt about who they were, but I didn't
share their confidence. I'd tried writing
my way through this, tried hiding from it,
held the slow-burning coals of self-loathing
between my teeth to get at the real pain of it.
The government's decision was in my hands
and it was time to accept what I'd asked for.

This plastic card that so many fought
for, that others fought to get out from
under. That goddamned *Act* still tearing
us apart. *Welcome to the club of gold*
teeth and free university! Say goodbye
to taxes, hello to fishing and hunting
without the crown keeping you down!
Add these to all the other misconceptions
that paint us red and white simultaneously.

I walk to the counter, open the drawer,
get a knife. Gut the envelope like a trout.
I don't read the letter, I'm too fucked up
by my greyscale face staring back at me,
even more by a smaller, translucent version
right next to it. Here's my face as I know it,
then as Canada sees me — ghost self to be
looked through, real but made up, Walbourne-
but-Gough, Newfoundlander-but-Mi'kmaw.

Tuckamore

Blunted by incessant wind, your stoop
and lean speak to decades of pressure
to take the knee, bog deep or cliff clung,
posing for photos, the reliance on otherness
to sell this island as worth stepping on.

Should some curious tourist walk
over you, your needled limbs will become
hardwood while their jaws gape, guffaws
of disbelief as Vibram and Gore-Tex
are selfied, instantly posted, unaware
of the cost of building your resilience.

Imagine the shock, the absolute awe
in their faces — their weatherproof gloves
useless, nothing to grasp up here but wind —
should you shift your shoulders, turn back
to face them, and say, *Do you mind?*

Dysregulation

Had to take a landscaping job. Fresh
home from Kelowna, MFA in hand,
I'd had enough of delivering high-end
furniture to the Okanagan's wealthy.

Mid-July heat. Sweat and sunscreen
pasted clipped grass and dead flies
to my forearms, shins and calves
scabbed from seventy-hour weeks
of flicked rocks, steel-toe boots
caked with chlorophyll and dog shit.

A customer lodged a complaint —
their lawn cut a half inch too short.
Boss got chewed out, so I was owed
a string of all the profane ways
I cost more than I'm worth.
His apology soon followed, emojis
to smooth things over, the promise
of a staff party that never happened,
complete with a BBQ and open bar.

A week later, I was sent back to trim
the affronted lawn. I texted my hesitation
to the boss but his go-to reply — *this is
a volume-based business* — said it all.
I opened the tailgate, jumped up
and filled up the mower. A voice
cut in — *no mistakes today, I'll be watching.*
I turned, gave a thumbs-up to a slammed door.

Maybe it's just the heat, or the hours,
or the boss, or the customers, me
caught up in it all with no way out.

Or maybe I just forgot. Doesn't matter —
another strip of lawn was cut too short.
I thought of the old barber's joke,
a lot harder to glue it back on!
Then, something fragile in me broke.

I swore, punched and kicked the truck,
pitched the lawnmower into the road.
My body so alive with rage — urge to kick
off the mirrors, toss the keys in a ditch,
text the boss a spiteful pic, finally yell
I quit — that I didn't know I was bawling.

The catalyst? Doesn't matter. A flat tire,
a breakup, one more rejection letter, any
mundane trouble could've triggered me.
I hadn't dealt with my shit. Decades of anger,
all my ugly unloved corners uncovered,
I slunk onto the pavement, hoping to
learn some lasting lesson beyond shame,
realizing I still had so much to let go of.

Retrofit

The setting was always sometime
in the future, but in that cyberpunk,
'80s sorta way. Trench coats, fingerless
gloves, fires in steel barrels. That air
of '80s cool that had no idea it should've
been self-conscious. Cowabunga.

There were always boards over
the windows of the houses, all
streetlights a faded orange, decades
of broken glass glinting on sidewalks.
Usually sirens in the distance.

The cool part was the hovering
car I'd always be in the back of,
looked kinda like an Eldorado
convertible. I'd hang over the edge,
watch the pavement's graffiti
pass under the car like a scroll.

There was a persistent, underlying
threat, my mother in danger. The driver
never turned his face toward me,
and she never took her eyes off him.

This dream had to recur a dozen times
before I realized this unknown man
was the one who left us, the one who'd
steered me into the future at odd angles
from some outdated story — here I am
again, all alone — a lazy plot, no character
development, just a self-serving dialogue
of hurt that was honest but never really true.

I Didn't Just Let This Happen

My first physical fight, only I have no idea it's coming. An older kid on the block calls out as I walk by, says to come in for a smoke. Happy to be asked, I walk inside, follow the older kid down to the finished basement. A couple old couches and end tables, ashtrays. A floor-model stereo. No music, though. I'm met with stares and silence, a half-dozen familiar faces wearing sort-of smiles, but with something hungry, something mean behind their teeth. My friends but nothing friendly about them. The older kid stands in front of the staircase, crosses his arms. Then, the new guy on the block steps forward, uncrosses his, slowly flexes his hands in and out of fists. My willingness to trust, to connect, leads me inside a crude circle of friends and old furniture, neither of which are asking me to sit down. I'm shoved into the new guy, who shoves me back. He swings and misses, I manage to get him into a headlock, hold him there and tell the circle I want no part of this. I'm so close to tears, but now isn't the time; I'd end up eaten alive. The new kid stops grunting and struggling and I let go, step back from him. Someone hands us each a lit cigarette, turns the music on.

Kuntew

Think of stone, its immovable load.
Now, this place nicknamed the Rock. How old
a mountain needs to be to fold, to roll
smooth — Gros Morne. We can't fathom the time
this took, running numbers, lines of zeros
to show each other how much we don't know.
The closest we come to this sense of time?
Elders, carrying bundles of story,

grandmothers, who've birthed those that birthed us,
aunties that transcend blood and surname —
this is how we become solid again.
Don't be bullied, don't rush this, escaping
Cabot's shadow is pure process. Look west,
breathe, plant your feet, and say *teliaq*.

Bastard

Mould stippled the bunk where
you were born, worn blankets gone
dank and stained like wood grain
and the place nearly unroofed,
letting all manner of weather in.
A true wonder either of us survived
your birth, and that bombastic
pastor calling you *foundling! foundling!*
claiming you a true miracle despite
your carnal start.

When I scoffed at this, he hissed
disbelief begets damnation and spat
at the stove for effect — the fool
knew I never owned anything
so warm as fire. He left in a fit
of hexes and raised fists, cursing
my flesh and all our names in order.

An old photograph of us — darkness
reaching in from the edges, plotting
to devour you from my arms, wrapped
in your burlap christening gown.
The priest fixed on you, wide-eyed
and hungry with belief, black robes
slack against his gaunt frame, praying
to hear the word *father* out of context.

I Didn't Just Let This Happen

Not Indigenous enough, not Mi'kmaw enough, too much Newfoundlander. My wallet full of cards tries to attach meaning to this body, but I'm occupying two spaces at once — colonizer and colonized. I can't seem to settle.

I'm busy trying to reckon with confederation, Qalipu enrolment, with childhood violence, with every time my self-destruction spilled onto the laps of others, with deforestation and oil exploration, with make-works and megaprojects turned boondoggles that we all saw coming, that we always see coming.

Too bad we're too starved for some quick relief to see past the next election cycle, erupting in petty jealousies over dental and medical benefits, too minimum wage and beleaguered by dollar stores and double-doubles and VLTs and so many crooked dreams of just making our bills with no waking end in sight.

I Still Dream of Moose

Still so real I can smell their mossy musk
and hot blood. Still shaking off bog muck,
bits of pitcher plants between their toes still
blessing their tracks with upside-down hearts.

But the light is no longer dusk, things don't
get quite so serious. Small groups still emerge
from treelines, still tiptoe and limbo around
town, but now the moose are fixed form.

Now, they cross the TCH, or the Viking Trail.
The downtown they trot through is usually past
the Sobeys, crossing Mt. Bernard Avenue
to hit the patch of woods by Glynmill Inn Pond.

There are no more sudden shifts to indoors,
no more shed antlers and growing gold teeth.
These days, my dream moose are content to be
moose, and my grandfather visits as himself.

Sometimes we're in the woods. Other times,
I'm in his kitchen and the kettle won't stop
whistling, or we're in Spruce Pond landing trout
hand over fist to fill our freezer for winter.

I love these visits, I hold them so dear I'm sure
he can feel my pulse, but I'm sure he also feels
how much I wish my grandmother would visit
with him, remind me of the sound of her voice.

Self-Doubt as Harvey Keitel as the Wolf

We're in downtown Corner Brook,
West Street. The Ultramar lot where
I spent so many years getting numb.
A white, '80s-model sports car pulls up,
the driver a knock-off of Harvey Keitel
as the Wolf, but in a white suit, cravat,
greyish blond, back-combed in wisps.

I approach the car, enamoured with
its gleam, how its outdatedness pales
in the face of its several vents, five-point-
star rims, modified body kit, its complete
lack of rust. Meanwhile, the Wolf chats
you up. I don't hear what's said, distracted
by this obsolete symbol of progress.

The Wolf gets out, opens the passenger
door, folds down the front seat, ushers
you into the back. I'm shocked, angry
with this stranger for being so bold,
ignoring me, shocked more when the Wolf
motions me to join, still holding the door
open, his eyes fixed on me like prey.

I sit, watch you watch the Wolf get back
into the car. Silence except for the creak
of the driver's-seat leather, the interior thick
with tension when you shift your body, lay
your hand on his white-suited shoulder
and squeeze. Still facing him, you tell me
to get out, I don't want to see this.

The Wolf adjusts the rear-view mirror,
stares into the back of my skull, sniffs,
turns to you, says, *You sure about that?*

First Date

My grandmother also kept journals.
My uncle told me about them, that Mom
had them a while, then my aunt had them
for some time after that. No one seems
to know where they are now.

As my grandmother watched the sun
set on her life prematurely, she also
kept eyes on Marie, the church volunteer
who cooked and cleaned their house
while Nan made peace with death.

Marie and my grandparents all got on
well, laughter and friendship came easy,
Nan always ready with a joke despite
her suffering. Seeing a possible life for Pop
after her own ended, she proposed a date.

I can't tell you what they wore, or how
their date went, what they ate, whether
either of them acknowledged how fucked up
their situation was, or the awkwardness
as he drove Marie home. All I know

is when he got home, he couldn't face
his wife without gratitude and heartbreak,
without guilt, confusion, or grief twisting
his face into knots, his sobs breaking
against their closed bedroom door.

How Do I Say This?

I downloaded an app to study Mi'kmaw,
tried to find a way back to language without
someone more Indigenous seeing my shame.
But I'm here, a Mi'kmaw Newfoundlander, trying.
Writing this mixed, frictioned experience in English.
Hoping to help anyone else who's this confused,
applying two-eyed seeing to the colonized self.
I know I belong to wind, belong to booming spray
that gnaws at granite cliffs, this stubborn island's
rough edges. I'm also cradled by the canoe I grew up
in, gliding on glassy ponds, trouting. Blueberries
and moose, the smell of black spruce in spring thaw.

I can't yet speak Mi'kmaw, but I can tell you
that I'll always be mixed, can't unadopt myself
from the family who raised me. I won't carry
a new-found shame, can't answer for its centuries
of colonial history. I have to carry these often-
conflicting selves, tend to them both with honesty.
I was once told, *You need to learn faster*, but I refuse
to rush. No one heals when pushed by someone else's
trauma. I want to respond with unflinching self-love
when questioned, reply *kesalul, kesaluloq*.

An app won't make me more Mi'kmaw,
but I'm done folding myself into someone
small out of fear. I'll keep repeating *Elmastukwek*
until the Blomidons, Cedar Cove, and Wee Ball
etch themselves into my skull. I'll whisper *Mi'kma'ki*
and *Ktaqmkuk* until they become synonymous, mouth
Maqtukwek until I'm no longer afraid it'll swallow me
whole. I want to sing *tia'm* and *atoqwa'su* to honour
what makes the marrow of my bones. *Meskeyi*
for the mistakes I'll make, *Wela'lioq* to those who've
shown me that a good heart is the way forward.

How's that puzzle coming?
Sure has a lot of sky.
— Dean Young

Acknowledgements and Thanks

This book was heavily inspired by dreams. The hopeful, waking sort born out of resisting the histories and realities that try to press and twist us into diminished versions of our true selves, but also the dreams our minds and hearts gift us while we sleep, where we are unconstrained by the physical and the dogmatic. Where magic is possible. And, of course, the kinds of dreams where these two veils overlap. Ultimately, though, maybe it's not about waking or sleeping. Maybe it's about yearning, about feeling. What do you yearn for? What are you unwilling to feel?

This book was lived, researched, and written on Mi'kma'ki.

Wela'lioq to Elder Calvin White and all the Newfoundland Mi'kmaq who fought, and are still fighting, the long fight to be seen, heard, and acknowledged. I wouldn't be who I am today without your efforts, and this island owes you all a great debt of thanks.

To this island for the good, bad, and ugly. Economy, food security, weather, and politics be damned, I've always felt like a tide pulled back home by the moon of this place. And to the constantly wise Cecily Nicholson for astutely reminding me that an island is only isolated on the surface.

Sue Sinclair — your eye, ear, and heart made space for my bundle of questions, feelings, and anxieties during this self-excavation — thank you for showing me that the risk was worthwhile.

Thom Vernon and Shannon Webb-Campbell for sharing your genuine magic with me along this PhD. To Dominique Béchard for *One Dog Town*, for such a sharp poetic eye. To Heather Nolan for always having a keen ear attuned to the pulse of this rock. To Terry Doyle and Greg the Dog for all the downtown walks and talks I didn't know I needed. To Taryn Kawaja for the downtown light-up see-saw adventure and Erin Bedford for the tiny champagne toast by the lake.

And, just like last time, there is a longer list of friends inhabiting my heart that is simply too long to include here. Wela'lioq, kesaluloq.

To the Goose Lane team — you've all taken such great care of me, and I couldn't ask for a better home for this important work.

I wish to acknowledge and thank the Canada Council for the Arts for financial support. Many thanks to all the editors of the journals and magazines who've believed in my work. I also want to express my sincere appreciation to those who've granted permission for my use of their words.

To my parents — I know some of these words aren't easy to sit with, but please know that with the honesty comes a tremendous lifelong love, respect, and friendship. Your constant reminder — *You'll always have a home with us* — is a tremendous privilege and the reason I'm still here.

Notes

I want to offer a note on my positionality. I refer to myself as mixed/adopted Mi'kmaq. I am a status member of the Qalipu First Nation, and my Mi'kmaq lineage comes from my adoptive father's family. Although the man I call Dad is not my father by blood, he's been in my life since I was two and has been everything a father could possibly be, and more, for the last thirty-nine years and counting. He *is* my father. I am incredibly proud to be his son and to have inherited the story of Crow Gulch. I see adoption as an advantage, rather than something that detracts from my "authenticity" as Mi'kmaq.

My adoption undermines the colonial practices of regulating belonging and exclusion sustained by the Indian Act, by conceptualizations of blood quantum alone as proof of Indigeneity. More importantly, and more powerfully, it means I have been chosen to be brought into my father's family. Adoption is a great privilege and keeps me connected to my community by love and gratitude, while also holding me responsible to my community. As a poet, I use my poetry as an attempt to give back to those who have chosen to accept me as Mi'kmaq.

My mother's family is mostly of settler descent, and her father was a Pentecostal pastor. My maternal grandfather, along with my grandmother and, later, his second wife, were missionaries in Hopedale and Natuashish, Labrador. On the surface, these family histories seem to be at odds. They are certainly an odd mix, but they are what I was born into, so I do my best to live forward with honesty about all parts of my family. An eye trained on both sides of my story, I hope to honour both the beauty and the mistakes, the humanity, of the people I come from. Mixed/adopted Mi'kmaw feels the most honest way I can express my position.

"The Arches" was first published in *Forget Magazine.*

"Attention," "I Visit My Grandfather with Sea Trout," and "Ten Percent" were first published in *Riddle Fence.*

"Another Visit from My Grandfather" was first published in *Newfoundland Quarterly.*

"Bastard" was first published in *G U E S T.*

"Canada's Happy Province" was a slogan used by the provincial government on a series of tourism posters in the late '50s and early '60s. It also appeared on Newfoundland and Labrador motor-vehicle licence plates issued in 1968.

The quote that begins "Corner Brook" comes from Dr. Neil White's *Company Towns: Corporate Order and Community*. It is an absolutely key text in understanding the social dynamics of this town, and the quote is used with the permission of the author.

"First Date" was first published in the *Fiddlehead*.

"Gerald Douglas Walbourne" first appeared in *Humber Mouths 2*.

"Herd" has been adapted to song in collaboration with Inuk professional classical singer, Deantha Edmunds. The poem, and Deantha's recording, have been rendered as a public art installation by visual artist Erienne Rennick, at Grenfell Campus School of Fine Arts. For more about Deantha and Erienne, visit deantha.ca and erienne-rennick-artist.squarespace.com.

"How Do I Say This?" first appeared in *Riddle Fence* and was awarded the 2022 Riddle Fence Poetry Prize. The Mi'kmaw words contained within the poem are approximately translated as follows: *Kesalul*—I love you, singular. *Kesaluloq*—I love you, plural. *Elmastukwek*—the Bay of Islands. *Mi'kma'ki*—traditional Mi'kmaw territory. *Ktaqmkuk*—the island of Newfoundland. *Maqtukwek*—the Humber River. *T'iam*—moose. *Atoqwa'su*—trout. *Meskeyi*—I am sorry. *Wela'lioq*—thank you, plural. Sincere gratitude to Dean Simon for his attention to the Mi'kmaw words in this poem, and his invaluable work toward Mi'kmaw language revival in Ktaqmkuk.

The poem references Etuaptmumk, or Two-Eyed Seeing, a concept that owes its origins to Elders Albert and Murdena Marshall, and Dr. Cheryl Bartlett. I first encountered Etuaptmumk in their 2012 article "Two-Eyed Seeing and other lessons learned within a co-learning journey of bringing together indigenous and mainstream knowledges and ways of knowing." The first printing of *Island* mistakenly omitted this reference. Meskeyi to Albert, Murdena, and Cheryl for my oversight. I called Elder Albert Marshall to own my mistake and, similar to my first call with Elder Calvin White, he met me with humour, then reassured me that no harm was done: Mi'kmaw knowledge couldn't be owned by any one person. This humility, generosity, and grace are an example I hope to live up to moving forward.

Both "I Still Dream of Moose" and its prequel poem from *Crow Gulch*, "I Dream of Moose," owe an obvious debt to John Steffler's poem "That Night We Were Ravenous."

"I Visit Margie with Moose Meat" references the mural *Crow Gulch*, created by Newfoundland Mi'kmaw artists Jordan Bennett and Marcus Gosse. While the mural isn't installed in Crow Gulch proper, it's a start and proof that art can generate dialogue and effect social change in the real world. Wela'lioq and big hugs to Jordan, Marcus, and Margie. This poem is published with Margie's consultation and permission.

"Kuntew" contains two Mi'kmaw words; the title itself, kuntew, refers to "stone(s)" or "rock(s)," while the word teliaq is defined as "that is so," or "that is true." The translations in "Kuntew" are sourced from *The Mi'kmaw Grammar of Father Pacifique: New Edition*, by Bernie Francis and John Hewson (2016). Francis and Hewson updated the original edition to use the Francis-Smith orthography used that is used in eastern Mi'kma'ki, including Ktaqmkuk.

The Mary Dalton quote from "My Uncouth Mouth" comes from the essay "A Book to Break Spells: *The Dictionary of Newfoundland English*" from her 2015 text, *Edge: Essays, Reviews, Interviews*, and is used with the permission of the author.

"Or, Perhaps You Have" was first published in *CV2*.

"Steep Steps Toward Home" first appeared in *Riddle Fence* and *Best Canadian Poetry 2019*.

The epigraph from "Ten Percent" comes from a Newfoundland provincial tourism website: https://newfoundlandlabrador.com/things-to-do/iceberg-viewing.

"This All Happened?" first appeared in *Janus Unbound: Journal of Critical Studies* and the title is a nod to Michael Winter's fictional memoir, *This All Happened.* The Thomas King quotation is from *The Inconvenient Indian* and is used with the permission of the author. The italicized text "I can lead you beside quiet waters" is a riff on Psalm 23:2, and "if you're gonna sing, sing 'em somethin' they can understand" is a quote attributed to Hank Williams.

"The Waves" was first published in *Grain.*

"We Could Fill a River" is based on my first conversation with Elder Calvin White, which has been a life-changing step toward healing. The poem is published with his consultation and permission and first appeared in the *Fiddlehead. The Country* is a 2018 documentary, co-produced and directed by Phyllis Ellis and James Yates, which highlights the voices of a handful of Mi'kmaq community members from southwestern Newfoundland. As Kelly Anne Butler, the documentary's screenwriter and third producer, explains, "One of the goals behind the film is to put a human face on the idea that the rest of Canada has around the idea of Newfoundland Mi'kmaq." A path that, thanks to *The Country,* this book can also work toward. https://www.facebook.com/TheCountryFilm.

The book's opening epigraphs come from Richard Siken's poem "Unfinished Duet," from his 2005 collection, *Crush,* and Mary Ruefle's 2012 text, *Madness, Rack, and Honey.* Both are used with the authors' permission.

The closing epigraph comes from Dean Young, excerpt from "Dragonfly" from *Fall Higher.* Copyright © 2011 by Dean Young. Reprinted with the permission of The Permissions Company, LLC on behalf of Copper Canyon Press, coppercanyonpress.org.

Douglas Walbourne-Gough is a poet and mixed/adopted status member of the Qalipu Mi'kmaq First Nation from Elmastukwek (the Bay of Islands), Ktaqmkuk (Newfoundland). He is the author of the chapbook *Colour Work* (Anstruther Press). His poetry has appeared in numerous publications, including *Best Canadian Poetry in English*, *Grain*, and the *Fiddlehead* and has won the Riddle Fence Poetry Prize.

Walbourne-Gough's debut collection, *Crow Gulch*, won the E.J. Pratt Poetry Award. It was also a finalist for NL Reads, the Derek Walcott Prize for Poetry, and the Raymond Souster Award, and was longlisted for the First Nation Communities READ Award. *Island* is his second book of poetry.